OUR
GRE★T
STATES

WHAT'S GREAT ABOUT

OREGON?

✳ Rebecca Felix

LERNER PUBLICATIONS ✳ MINNEAPOLIS

CONTENTS

OREGON WELCOMES YOU! ✳ 4

Content Consultant: David Peterson del Mar,
Associate Professor, Portland State University

Lerner Publications Company
A division of Lerner Publishing Group, Inc.
241 First Avenue North
Minneapolis, MN 55401 USA

For reading levels and more information, look
up this title at www.lernerbooks.com.

Main body text set in ITC Franklin Gothic Std
Book Condensed 12/15.
Typeface provided by Adobe Systems.

Library of Congress Cataloging-in-Publication
Data

Felix, Rebecca, 1984–
    What's great about Oregon? / by
Rebecca Felix.
        pages   cm. — (Our great states)
    Includes index.
    Audience: Ages 7–11.
    ISBN 978-1-4677-3866-8 (lib. bdg. :
alk. paper) — ISBN 978-1-4677-6090-4
(pbk.) — ISBN 978-1-4677-6268-7 (EB
pdf)
    1. Oregon—Juvenile literature. I. Title.
F876.3.F45 2015
979.5—dc23   2014027046

Manufactured in the United States of America
1 – PC – 12/31/14

OREGON Welcomes You!

Bright blue lakes and rushing waterfalls sparkle amid thick forests. Ferns and evergreens grow strong and tall under frequently rainy skies. Can you smell the crisp mountain air? You're in Oregon! This state has many beautiful sights. People ski and hike in the snowy Cascade Mountains. Sea lions bark in sea caves, and gray whales can be spotted off the Pacific Coast. Visit and see for yourself. But first read on to find out about ten things that make Oregon great!

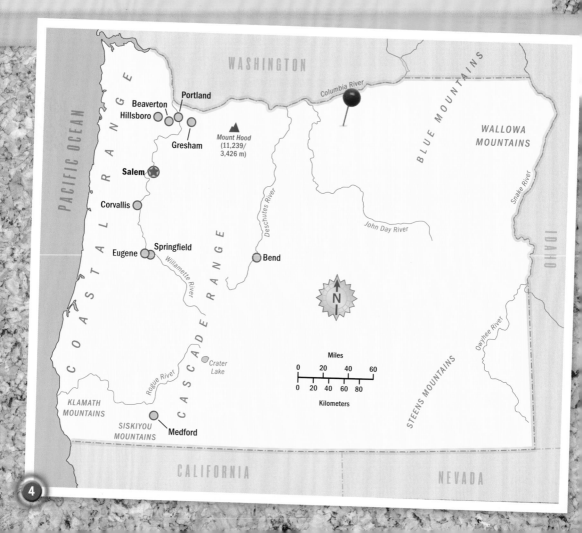

Explore Oregon's forests and all the places in between. Just turn the page to find out all about the BEAVER STATE. >

PORTLAND

> Portland is Oregon's biggest city. Hop on a rentable bicycle and pedal your way around the town. You won't want to miss Portland's Washington Park. It is a huge park inside the city. Your first stop is the giant playground. It has slides, a castle, bridges, and ramps. The International Rose Test Garden is also in the park. Breathe in the sweet smell of more than ten thousand rose bushes. Then walk through forests from around the world at the World Forestry Center.

Continue your Portland adventure at the city's museums. Watch a laser light show at the Oregon Museum of Science and Industry. You can also tour a real US Navy submarine there. At the Portland Children's Museum, mold clay masterpieces or create construction projects in the museum's garage. Then head outside. The museum has a huge outdoor exhibit. Explore trails through a meadow. Then build a log shelter at the campsite station. You can also swing and climb through the maze of branches on the giant climbing tree.

OREGON TRAIL

In the 1840s, people in the Midwest region of the United States struggled in an economic depression. They heard stories of land in Oregon that was good for farming. In 1843, approximately one thousand people set out on a trek to Oregon. Their path came to be known as the Oregon Trail. Many would travel it. It was a long and dangerous route. Many people died. Those who made it to Oregon settled the land. More people arrived using the Oregon Trail in the following decades.

Tour the USS *Blueblack*, a real US Navy submarine that was in use for thirty-one years, at the Oregon Museum of Science and Industry.

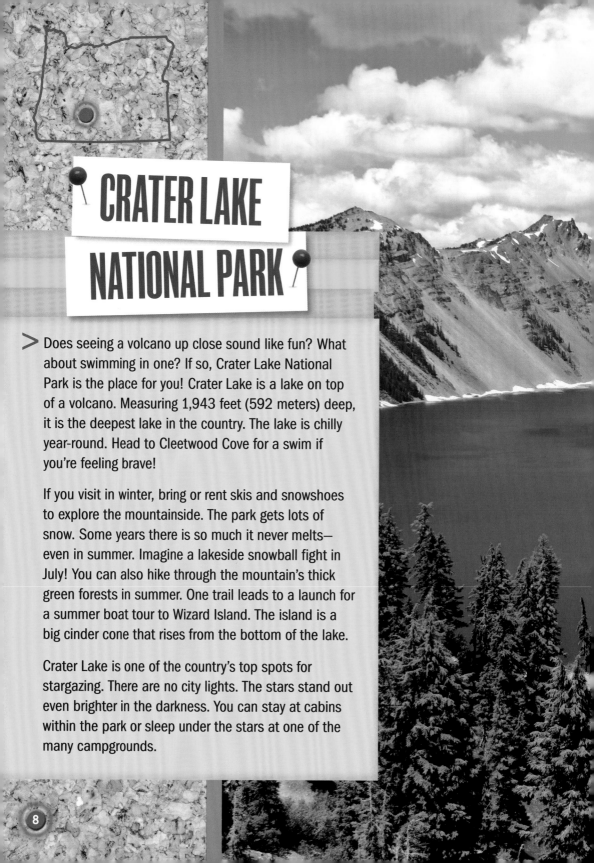

CRATER LAKE NATIONAL PARK

> Does seeing a volcano up close sound like fun? What about swimming in one? If so, Crater Lake National Park is the place for you! Crater Lake is a lake on top of a volcano. Measuring 1,943 feet (592 meters) deep, it is the deepest lake in the country. The lake is chilly year-round. Head to Cleetwood Cove for a swim if you're feeling brave!

If you visit in winter, bring or rent skis and snowshoes to explore the mountainside. The park gets lots of snow. Some years there is so much it never melts—even in summer. Imagine a lakeside snowball fight in July! You can also hike through the mountain's thick green forests in summer. One trail leads to a launch for a summer boat tour to Wizard Island. The island is a big cinder cone that rises from the bottom of the lake.

Crater Lake is one of the country's top spots for stargazing. There are no city lights. The stars stand out even brighter in the darkness. You can stay at cabins within the park or sleep under the stars at one of the many campgrounds.

Hike and picnic on Wizard Island while exploring Crater Lake National Park.

CRATER LAKE'S CLEAR WATER

Crater Lake's volcano last erupted more than seven thousand years ago. When it did, the top part of the volcano caved in to form a crater. For many years, rain and melting snow filled the crater. The water is so clear you can see down almost 100 feet (31 m). Crater Lake's water is a deep, bright blue because the water is from precipitation. This means the water is pure, clear water. It has no sand, algae, or pollution.

FAMILY FUN CENTER

Mini golf is just one of the many activities at the Family Fun Center.

> Wilsonville is home to the Family Fun Center. You can soar down a zip line, try mini golf, ride rides, and more all at this park! Buckle in to the Soaring Eagle. It is a seated zip line ride. It pulls riders backward and up 75 feet (23 m) in the air. Then the riders are flung forward on the cable. Fly over the park at high speeds!

Next, jump into a go-kart with a parent or an older sibling and race. Then battle your family in a round of mini golf. If you have energy left, hit the batting cages, balance on the rope obstacle course, or climb the rock wall. Then take a pizza or ice-cream break. The park's restaurant has life-sized, mechanical cartoon characters that perform while you eat! When you're finished eating, there's more fun indoors. Compete in extreme laser tag or check out more than one hundred games in the two-story arcade.

Bump into friends or family members in the Family Fun Center's bumper boats.

OREGON COAST WHALE WATCHING

> Imagine zipping out to sea on a small, inflatable boat. You spot a great mist coming from the surface. It's a whale spouting air and water! And it is huge—many times bigger than your boat. If this sounds like an adventure, whale watching on the Oregon coast is for you.

Gray whales are the most common whales to see on the Oregon coast. Approximately eighteen thousand of them migrate past the state each winter and summer. About two hundred stay near the state for most of the year. These are called resident whales. Depoe Bay is known as Oregon's whale-watching capital. Several boats here will take you to see the whales up close. Many whales are curious. They often approach the boat. Some even get close enough for you to touch! As you ride out to sea looking for whales, don't forget to watch for other sea life. Sea lions, seals, porpoises, and many other animals also live in the coastal waters.

GRAY WHALE MIGRATION

Gray whales feed in cold Alaskan waters in the summer. But as winter approaches, they head to warmer waters. Around December or January, gray whales travel south. They pass the Oregon coast along the way. They migrate to areas near Southern California and Mexico. There, they will give birth in the warmer waters. Then they travel back up north with their calves between March and June. They eat in Alaskan waters until the next winter, when they migrate south again.

Watch for sea lions perched on the rocky Oregon coast.

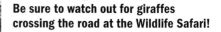

Be sure to watch out for giraffes crossing the road at the Wildlife Safari!

WILDLIFE SAFARI

> Most safaris take place in Africa. But Oregon also has them! The town of Winston is home to the Wildlife Safari park. Here, animals live on more than 600 acres (243 hectares) of grassland and forest. You can see them from your family car! Lions, tigers, cheetahs, and bears are all in the park. Don't forget to look up! Elephants and giraffes might cross your path. Camels, zebras, and elk could look into your car windows. Throughout most of the park, you must keep car windows rolled up for safety. But not in the Asia exhibit. Buy cups of food to feed Asian deer, yaks, and cranes. They will come up to the car and eat right out of your hand!

For the ultimate animal experience, try sleeping near the animals. You and your family can stay overnight on special days in the Safari Overnight Adventure Camp. See a show about nocturnal animals. Guided hikes take place at night. Then get cozy in your tent and listen. You might fall asleep to the sound of roaring lions!

Feed an East African crowned crane in the Wildlife Safari's Asia exhibit.

The tree houses at Out'n'About Treehouse Treesort even have electricity!

OUT'N'ABOUT TREEHOUSE TREESORT

> Have you ever seen a village in the trees? Visit the Out'n'About Treehouse Treesort in Cave Junction! Stay overnight in tree houses connected by rope bridges. The tree houses have electric lights, beds, bathrooms, and kitchens. Don't sleep in too late! Tons of activities await. Learn to climb trees on a rope-climbing course. Play on one of the resort's five big swings. Or test out the Giant Tarzan Swing. First, a guide hooks you onto a 50-foot (15 m) rope. Then you use handles to pull yourself high in the trees. When the guide says it's time, you pull the handle. You'll swing down through the trees!

For more airborne fun, whiz around on one of ten zip line courses. Did you spot the horses from above? You'll also find a ranch and a riding stable here. Back at camp, swim in a freshwater pool fed by a river. Or take a class on how to build a tree house or make the perfect s'more. This will come in handy at the resort's nightly bonfire.

Roast marshmallows each evening at the Out'n'About Treehouse Treesort bonfire.

Kayak in Bend's Elk Lake.

BEND

> Bend is a city packed with outdoor fun! It has a variety of landscapes. On land, Smith Rock State Park has huge rock formations perfect for climbing. Guides offer lessons for all ages. In winter, snow tube at Wanoga Sno-Park or down Mount Bachelor. You can also ski, snowboard, or go for a dogsled ride. Sit back and get cozy as a professional musher guides a team of dogs to pull you!

Enjoy Bend's rivers, lakes, mountains, desert, and forests. Start your outdoor tour of Bend on the water. Go fishing at Shevlin Park. Its pond is for kids only! Next, strap on a life jacket and get ready for a rush! Sun Country Tours offers family rafting trips. Raft around islands made of lava. Glide through a canyon or past an ancient forest. Kayak, canoe, or even float down the river on a tube.

OREGON'S REGIONS

Much of Oregon is covered in forests. Trees cover the Cascade Mountains, which run north and south inland from the coast. The land closest to the sea consists of plains, pastures, and rocky cliffs. On the other side of the Cascade Mountains is the Willamette Valley. The southeast corner of the state is high desert. The Deschutes River runs through the middle of the state. The Snake River carves out a gorge and canyon on the Idaho border.

OREGON CAVES NATIONAL MONUMENT

> You can explore underground at Oregon Caves National Monument. The cave is located on the side of a mountain in the Siskiyou range. It has four levels of sparkly, jagged, and swirling rock formations. Get ready to duck and twist! You'll find many stairs to climb on the cave tour. Passages between chambers can be very small. But the sights are worth the challenge.

Stalactites form and hang from the ceiling. Stalagmites grow up from the cave floor. There are swirling and bubbled rock walls. The cave and some of its formations took hundreds of thousands of years to form! Your guide will tell you more about the cave and the fossils and creatures you might see. Visit in summer for a candlelight tour. See the cave as early explorers would have seen it. Dress warm, even in summer. The cave stays at approximately the same temperature as a refrigerator all year. For an extra-spooky experience, visit near Halloween. Hear ghost stories as you walk among dangling bats!

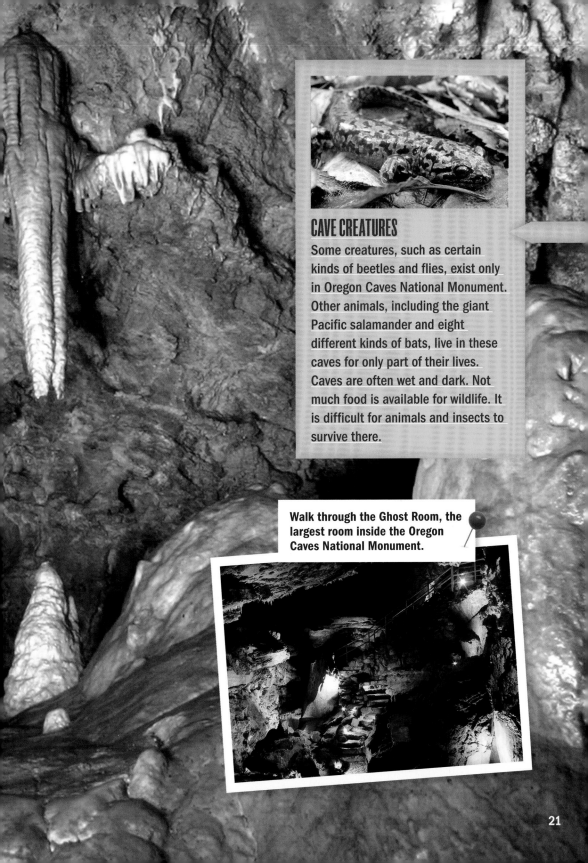

CAVE CREATURES

Some creatures, such as certain kinds of beetles and flies, exist only in Oregon Caves National Monument. Other animals, including the giant Pacific salamander and eight different kinds of bats, live in these caves for only part of their lives. Caves are often wet and dark. Not much food is available for wildlife. It is difficult for animals and insects to survive there.

Walk through the Ghost Room, the largest room inside the Oregon Caves National Monument.

OREGON AQUARIUMS

> You can sleep next to sharks at the Portland Aquarium! Sleep with the Sharks is a night tour. It ends with a sleepover right next to one of the exhibits. You might wake up next to a shark! In the morning, you can join the aquarium staff. Watch them check on the animals. You may see the staff feed jellyfish, seahorses, or the hungry sharks you woke up next to!

Next, visit the the Oregon Coast Aquarium to see some of the animals that live along the Oregon coast. The famous orca whale from the film *Free Willy* once lived here! See a broadnose sevengill shark. Go behind the scenes to meet—and get a kiss from—a sea lion or a seal! Make your next stop the Coastal Waters exhibit. Here, you can see moon jellyfish and bat stars. To meet the animals under water, sign up for face-to-face snorkeling. A dive guide will take you on a swim inside the tanks with fish and sea kelp.

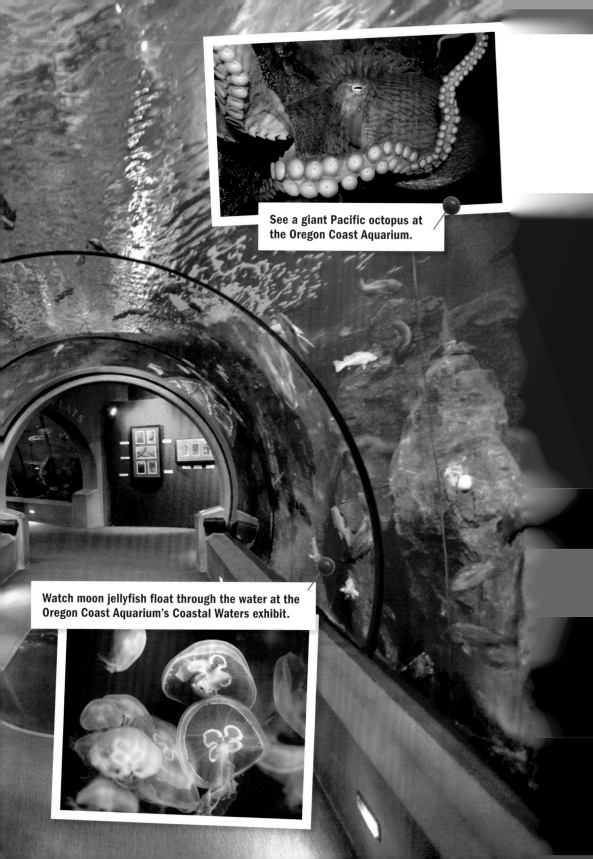

See a giant Pacific octopus at the Oregon Coast Aquarium.

Watch moon jellyfish float through the water at the Oregon Coast Aquarium's Coastal Waters exhibit.

After a day of rafting, set up a tent and camp in Hells Canyon.

HELLS CANYON

> Hells Canyon is a gorge on Oregon's eastern border. The Snake River runs between the canyon walls, along the border of Oregon and Idaho. Hells Canyon is more than 1 mile (1.6 kilometers) deep in many places. It is the deepest gorge in North America. Explore the canyon's towering walls, rushing rapids, and surrounding forest by raft, jet boat, or horse.

Winding Waters River Expeditions offers summer camping, rafting, and horseback riding trips through the canyon. Rafting trips are three to five days. They include days of floating, rafting, swimming, and fishing. Nights end with a bonfire and camping along the river. The Paddles to Saddles trip lasts for seven days. Raft the rapids for four days. Then spend the last three days riding through the Eagle Cap Wilderness. Here you'll see some of the highest peaks in Oregon. Want to experience the canyon at a faster pace? Hop on a Hells Canyon Adventures boat. Hold on tight! These jet boats cut through rapids and whiz past the jagged canyon walls.

YOUR TOP TEN

You just read about ten great things to do in Oregon. What would make your must-do list if you were planning an Oregon trip? Write down your top ten choices. You can even make them into a book just like this one. Find and print images from the Internet. Or draw your own pictures to use in your book. Have fun planning your trip!

Take a rafting trip down the Snake River while visiting Hells Canyon.

OREGON BY MAP

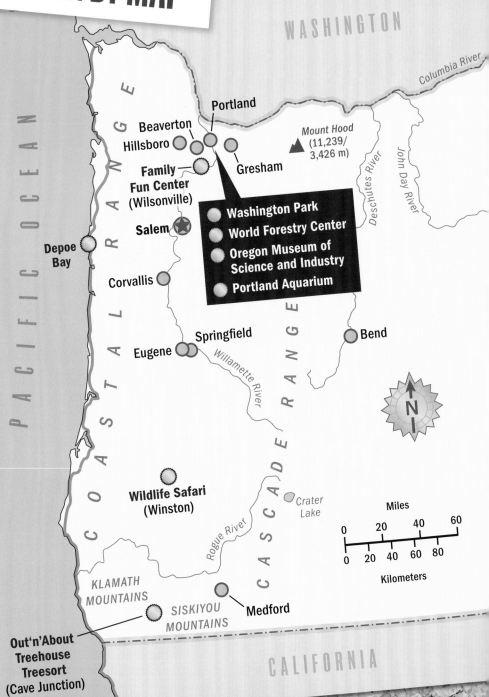

WASHINGTON

Columbia River

PACIFIC OCEAN

COASTAL RANGE

CASCADE RANGE

Portland

Beaverton
Hillsboro

**Family
Fun Center**
(Wilsonville)

Salem

Gresham

Mount Hood
(11,239/
3,426 m)

Deschutes River

John Day River

Washington Park

World Forestry Center

Oregon Museum of
Science and Industry

Portland Aquarium

Depoe
Bay

Corvallis

Springfield

Eugene

Willamette River

Bend

Wildlife Safari
(Winston)

Crater
Lake

Rogue River

KLAMATH
MOUNTAINS

SISKIYOU
MOUNTAINS

Medford

**Out'n'About
Treehouse
Treesort**
(Cave Junction)

CALIFORNIA

N

Miles
0   20   40   60

0   20   40   60   80

Kilometers

> MAP KEY

Capital city

City

Point of interest

Highest elevation

State border

Pacific Coast Highway

BLUE MOUNTAINS

Hells Canyon

WALLOWA MOUNTAINS

IDAHO

Snake River

Owyhee River

STEENS MOUNTAINS

NEVADA

STATE OF OREGON

THE UNION

1859

Visit www.lerneresource.com to learn more about the state flag of Oregon.

OREGON FACTS

NICKNAME: The Beaver State

SONG: "Oregon, My Oregon" by J. A. Buchanan and Henry B. Murtagh

MOTTO: "She Flies with Her Own Wings"

FLOWER: Oregon grape

TREE: Douglas fir

BIRD: western meadowlark

ANIMAL: beaver

DATE AND RANK OF STATEHOOD: February 14, 1859; the 33rd state

CAPITAL: Salem

AREA: 97,048 square miles (251,353 sq. km)

AVERAGE JANUARY TEMPERATURE: 32°F (0°C)

AVERAGE JULY TEMPERATURE: 66°F (19°C)

POPULATION AND RANK: 3,930,065; 27th (2013)

MAJOR CITIES AND POPULATIONS: Portland (603,106), Eugene (157,986), Salem (157,429), Gresham (108,956), Hillsboro (95,327), Beaverton (92,680)

NUMBER OF US CONGRESS MEMBERS: 5 representatives; 2 senators

NUMBER OF ELECTORAL VOTES: 7

NATURAL RESOURCES: forests, minerals, water, fertile soils

AGRICULTURAL PRODUCTS: beef cattle, hay, milk, timber, wheat

MANUFACTURED GOODS: computer and electronic products, metal products, food products, machinery, paper products, transportation equipment, wood products

STATE HOLIDAYS AND CELEBRATIONS: Portland Rose Festival, Oregon State Fair

The Royal Rosarians Foundation
Ambassadors of Goodwill for the City of Roses

GLOSSARY

algae: small, rootless plants that often grow in water

cinder cone: a deposit around a volcanic vent formed by rock fragments during eruption and shaped like a cone with a crater on top

economic depression: a time when a country's economy struggles and many people lose their money

erupt: to send out hot lava, rock, and steam in a sudden explosion

exhibit: an object or collection of objects on display

fossil: a trace of an animal or plant that is millions of years old and preserved in or as rock

gorge: a canyon with steep walls

migrate: the movement of animals from one area to another at a certain time of year

musher: the person who drives a dogsled

nocturnal: happening, or active, at night

precipitation: water that falls from the sky in the form of rain, snow, sleet, or hail

stalactite: a mineral deposit that is shaped like an icicle and hangs from a cave ceiling

stalagmite: a mineral deposit that sticks up from a cave floor and forms from the drips of a stalactite

LERNER

SOURCE

Expand learning beyond the printed book. Download free, complementary educational resources for this book from our website, www.lerneresource.com.

FURTHER INFORMATION

America's Story: Oregon
http://www.americaslibrary.gov/es/or/es_or_subj.html
Read information about the history of Oregon. Then click through fun stories and images about the state, including stories on sand castles, volcanoes, and fishing.

Aronin, Miriam. *How Many People Traveled the Oregon Trail? And Other Questions about the Trail West.* Minneapolis: Lerner Publications, 2012. Read about the Oregon Trail, a route used by many pioneers who traveled to Oregon and settled the land.

Brown, Cynthia Light. *Geology of the Pacific Northwest: Investigate How the Earth Was Formed with 15 Projects.* White River Junction, VT: Nomad, 2011. Create fun projects and learn how earthquakes, volcanoes, and other geologic forces created the Pacific Northwest's physical features.

Hart, Joyce. *Oregon.* New York: Marshall Cavendish Benchmark, 2012. Learn more about the state of Oregon, including its history, important people, and geography.

Oregon Wild: Oregon's Fish and Wildlife
http://www.oregonwild.org/wildlife
Read about Oregon's landscapes and the wildlife that live in them, as well as updates on efforts to conserve and protect certain animals and habitats.

State Facts for Students: Oregon
http://www.census.gov/schools/facts/oregon.html
Get fast facts about Oregon, such as how many kids ages eight to twelve live there and how many amusement parks and zoos are in the state.

INDEX

PHOTO ACKNOWLEDGMENTS

The images in this book are used with the permission of: © Andrey Tarantin/Shutterstock Images, p. 1; NASA, pp. 2–3; © Laura Westlund/Independent Picture Service, pp. 4, 26–27; © Mogens Trolle/Shutterstock Images, p. 5 (top); © Joyce Marrero/Shutterstock Images, p. 5 (bottom); US National Archives and Records Administration, p. 6; © Nagel Photography/Shutterstock Images, pp. 6–7; Robert Gaskin, p. 7; © Lindsay Douglas/Shutterstock Images, pp. 8–9; © William Perugini/Shuterstock Images, p. 9 (top); © Matthew Connolly/Shutterstock Images, p. 9 (bottom); © Andrey Kuzmin/Shutterstock Images, p. 10; © Gow27/Shuterstock Images, pp. 10–11; © John Le Blanc/Shutterstock Images, p. 11; Merrill Gosho/National Oceanic and Atmospheric Administration, pp. 12–13; © Steve Estvanik/Shutterstock Images, p. 13 (bottom); © Fuse/Thinkstock, p. 13 (top); © Wollertz/Shutterstock Images, pp. 14, 15; Justin Brockie, pp. 14–15; © Wood Wheatcroft/Aurora Open/Corbis, pp. 16, 16–17; © Phil McDonald/Shutterstock Images, p. 17; © tusharkoley/Shutterstock Images, p. 18; Ennetws, pp. 18–19; © Paula Cobleigh/Shutterstock Images, p. 19; Roger Brandt/National Park Service, pp. 20–21; © Jeffrey Marsten, p. 21 (top); National Park Service, p. 21 (bottom); © Dennis Frates/Alamy, pp. 22–23; © Jason Mintzer/Shutterstock Images, p. 23 (top); © Iakov Filimonov/Shutterstock Images, p. 23 (bottom); © Log Carter/Shutterstock Images, p. 24; © Jeffrey T. Kreulen/Shutterstock Images, pp. 24–25; © Robynrg/Shutterstock Images, p. 25; © nicoolay/iStockphoto, p. 27; © Robert Crum/Shutterstock Images, p. 29 (top right); © Krzysztof Wiktor/Shutterstock Images, p. 29 (top left); © Victoria Ditkovsky/Shutterstock Images, p. 29 (bottom right); © Rigucci/Shutterstock Images, p. 29 (bottom left).

Cover: The images in this book are used with the permission of: © Robin Winkelman/Dreamstime.com (sea lion); © Steve Wanke/Taxi/Getty Images (Portland); © Connie Coleman/Photographer's Choice RF/Getty Images (Crater Lake); © Out'n'About Treesort LLC (treehouse); © Laura Westlund/Independent Picture Service (map); © iStockphoto.com/fpm (seal); © iStockphoto.com/vicm (pushpins); © iStockphoto.com/benz190 (corkboard).